PRIORSLEE
Remembered

Researched and written by

ALLAN FROST

AJF Desk Top Publishing

By the same author

The Story of Donnington and its Parish Church (1979)
The Stracyl of Unity (fantasy novel) (1991)

All rights reserved.
No part of this book may be
reproduced or transmitted in any form or by any means,
electronic or mechanical, including photocopying,
recording or any information storage and retrieval system,
without permission in writing from the publisher.

This book is sold subject to the conditions that it shall not,
by way of trade or otherwise, be lent, re-sold, hired out
or otherwise circulated without the publisher's prior consent
in any form of binding or cover other than that in which
it is published and without a similar condition including
this condition being imposed on the subsequent purchaser.

© Allan John Frost 1993

ISBN 1 872989 02 0

Designed and typeset by AJF Desk Top Publishing
1 Buttermere Drive, Priorslee, Telford, Shropshire, TF2 9RE, England

Printed by Graphics & Print Ltd
Unit A13, Stafford Park 15, Telford, Shropshire, TF3 3BB

British Library Cataloguing-in-Publication Data
A CIP catalogue record for this book is available from the British Library

CONTENTS

Foreword	5
Dolly Harris	7
George Leese	14
Millie Parry	21
Billy Pascall	30
Frank Dixon	39
Mixed Memories	49

The maps used throughout this book are extracts from the Ordnance Survey 1889, 1903 and 1938 Editions.

FOR DOROTHY

*in appreciation of her unlimited patience
(and resignation) during my many hours of research.*

FOREWORD

Telford has, in recent years, been the subject of an abundance of local histories, often of the Ironbridge Gorge.

This book reveals community life in old Priorslee to have been a fascinating combination of agricultural and industrial co-existence.

During my research I have been impressed by the hospitality, enthusiasm and willingness to reveal even the smallest detail of life as it was before Telford New Town was conceived. Several of the people interviewed either had very little to add to this collection or they wished to remain anonymous; their comments have been combined to form the last chapter of this book.

Sincere thanks are due to those who have lent me their treasured photographs, other historic documents and rare memorabilia, whatever condition they have been in; they are all invaluable records.

I hope you enjoy reading it as much as I enjoyed listening to the revelations of those whose memories are recorded here.

Finally, I am very much indebted to the management of NEC Technologies (UK) Ltd at Castle Farm Campus in Priorslee for their most generous contribution towards the printing costs of this book.

Allan Frost
Priorslee, Telford

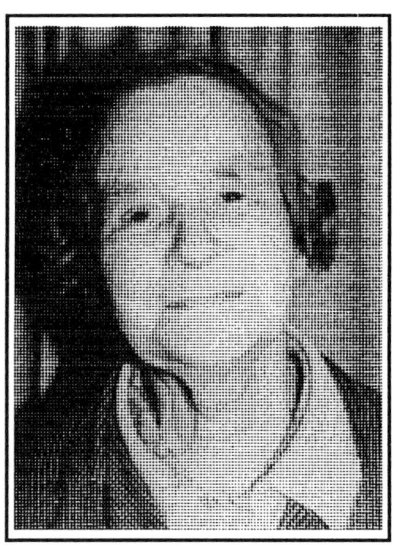

Dolly Harris

Dorothy 'Dolly' Harris (née Franks) was born on 7th June 1908 in Wellington Road, Donnington. She was fostered at 8 years old to a Mr and Mrs Biddulph and lived in St Georges and Hollinswood during the years prior to her marriage to Isaac Harris, who died in 1991. She has lived in a small Duke of Sutherland cottage in Donnington for over 50 years.

Priorslee School was on the ground opposite and slightly above the Sneds Hill Methodist Chapel and between Priorslee Road and Church Road. I was there when the big strike was on around 1920, before the General Strike of 1926.

There used to be a big porch where you put all your clothes in and it had a big fire. In the winter we all used to huddle around this fire – there was no central heating in the school. The toilets were outside, and if you wanted to go you had to cross the yard, whatever the weather.

Like other children at the time we played with tops, hoops and skipping ropes. The hoops were made of iron and rolled along using a pot hook. We didn't really have any proper games at school: we were there to learn and learn we did! Not like today. Mind you, we weren't given any homework to do; conditions at home weren't really suitable for study.

I remember my friend Rhoda, who was top of the class, helping me to do some sums during the lesson: she passed the answers along under the desks for me to copy. She used to earn many a sixpence that way!

Mr Upton from St Georges was the headmaster – he was crippled up almost double, and he had a cane. If you talked in school he'd give you six of the best. If we had to hold our hand out to be beaten we sometimes whipped it away at the last moment when the cane was coming down, but you couldn't escape!

Miss Mollineux, Mrs Turner and Mr Upton's daughter were the teachers there, together with Mr Price, also from St Georges; they were quite good.

Mrs Corbett used to make soup for us schoolchildren; I can see her now, coming across the road with these enamel buckets and the split peas bobbing on the top. You had a bowl of soup and a big lump of bread for one penny.

I went to St Peter's Church for Sunday School in the morning, then on to the church service afterwards. Not a lot went on at the church in those days. The Vicarage was in the same road as the church, opposite the Priorslee Institute and next to the school.

Priorslee Institute, a wooden hut, was in Church Road near to the Church and quite a few games, like cricket and tennis, were played in the grounds. Me and my friend used to look in the hedges for all the lost tennis balls and keep them for ourselves. The Institute was used for dinners and all sorts of community activities. I think there it had a bit of a library, but I'm not sure.

Cricket was also played on a field below the Lion Inn, not far from where the Priorslee Hall Lodge was. There was a large mulberry tree by the field, the only one in the district, and my friends and I occasionally climbed the tree and threw the berries down to eat later.

Mr Wallace Tart, rather badly crippled, used to keep a little wooden shop by the railway line below the Pigeon Box, and his house was on the other side of the road. His parents put him in the

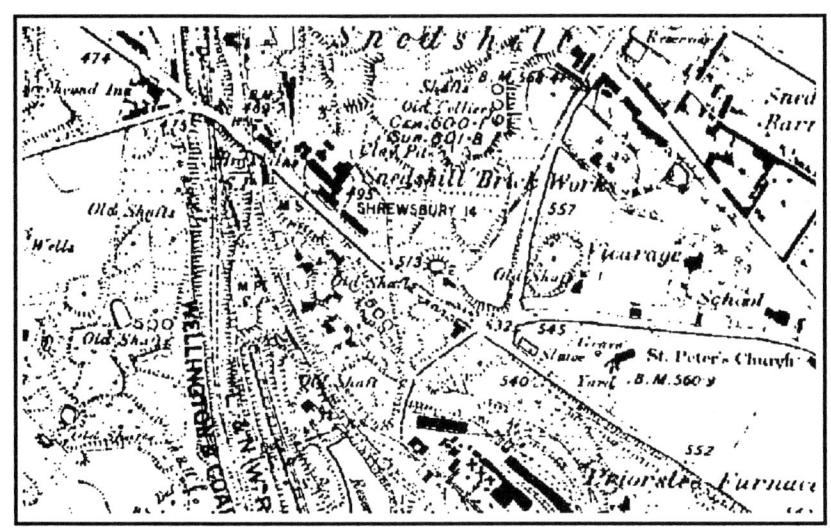

Location of St Peter's Church, Priorslee

The Church of St Peter, Priorslee c. 1900

shop to give him something to do. His father was watchman at the Priorslee Furnaces in later life after he retired. (Mr Biddulph, one of my foster parents, was also a watchman at the furnaces.) The shop sold practically anything – sweets (two ounces for a penny), tea, sugar and all sorts of groceries.

The Teagues kept the Pigeon Box when I lived up at Priorslee. Later they went to keep the 'Vic' next to Whiteford's shop in Oakengates. (My husband worked at Whiteford's for 16½ years. When he left his wages were 42s 6d – £2.12½p – a week!) Nellie Teague used to have a horse: we used to think they were so well off for having this horse! I think they also had a farm not far away down Teagues Lane which ran from the Priorslee Road to the Woodhouse Pit.

There were some old miners' barrack houses near the Pigeon Box. Some of the people living there were called Leylands and their son went to school with me. When we lived at Hollinswood we had to get our water for the wash-house at the back from a tap at the roadside, each tap serving about 20 houses. Each family did their washing on different days to avoid everyone being in there at the same time. I can still remember all the dolly tubs! Youngsters today don't know they're born!

The milkman delivered milk from a large can or churn from which he ladled it out into one of our large jugs.

Workers' houses were lit with candles or oil lamps and had a coal fireplace. Coal was very cheap and often free to miners working in the pits. I remember paying 3s 6d – 17½p – for a sack of coal and a sack of nutty slack. Nutty slack was coal dust with small bits of coal left in it. It was delivered by Chetwood's, a coalmerchant at Hollinswood, on horsedrawn carts. They'd have a 'chain horse' to help the main horse haul the cart up the Hollinswood bank, and after the cart had reached the top Mr Chetwood would unharness the chain horse and give it a slap to send it back, all on its own, to the field by the Priorslee furnaces where they had a small coal depot.

Most houses had outside toilets, usually two-seaters shared between two families and with old newspapers cut into rough squares to act as toilet paper. You used to have to sing if you were in there to warn the unwary! If it was dark we had to take a lantern or candle in with us. These toilets weren't connected to a sewage system, so the night soil men came in the hours of darkness to empty them out. Those were the days!

Looking back, the place was a bit of a tip because they didn't have dustbins then, so rubbish was usually burned and the ashes were scattered over the gardens.

There wasn't really much to do apart from going to the Pictures – the Grosvenor at Oakengates. I can remember it being built, and I can remember it being pulled down. It's a shame. The Oakengates Town Hall (as was) in Market Street also used to be a cinema. Seats there cost 2d and 9d depending where you sat.

I sometimes went to Priorslee Hall on errands for my employer Champion Jones who lived at Ivy House. He had an important job at the Lilleshall Company and I worked for him as a domestic servant and childminder. That was most girls did when they left school and before they got married. They were expected to give up work altogether after marriage. I remember that he was very tall and very thin, and rode a Douglas motorcycle. His knees almost reached to his chin when he sat on it.

Obviously, I wasn't allowed beyond the kitchen and it used to fascinate me, looking up at all these pheasants and other creatures hanging from the ceiling, and maggots dropping down from them! I can also remember lots of stone jars on the floor. They were filled with flour and all sorts of ingredients. The kitchens were absolutely enormous.

I can remember when Mr Freeston came to the Hall; Mr McKinley kept it before Mr Freeston. I never liked Mr Freeston, he was rather a hard man.

There was a row of cottages in the village and I also had to run errands to a Mr Green who lived in one of the big houses near there. He also had flitches and different things hanging up in his kitchen, as well as maggots falling down and crawling everywhere. I can't see how they managed to eat anything like that in those days!

I left Priorslee well over 60 years ago, but I can remember Freeston Avenue being built. Mrs Margerrison (the local chemist's mother) lived in one of the 48 houses in the Long Row which was demolished to make room for them. The Cotton family (16 of them altogether) lived in one of the old two-bedroomed houses in the same row. Mrs Cotton had a son who lost his wife, and I think she reared his two children as well! Jack, the youngest son, was valet to Jack Hulbert, husband of Dame Cicely Courtneidge, the famous actress and musical performer. We thought we knew when Jack Cotton had been home because his mother, who was very tall, used to wear a different big hat with flowing feathers, and we all believed they had come straight from Cicely.

Another group of houses called Short Row ran off Long Row, and they were demolished as well. *(Both Rows belonged to the groups of housing known collectively as Snedshill Barracks.)*

The old Post Office had double bay windows and was next to the Lion Inn. It wasn't much of a place, Post Offices often weren't in those days, it had a little room at the front where business was conducted. Stone House, on the other side of the Lion Inn, was owned, I believe, by the Lilleshall Company and occupied at the time by Mr Kenworthy, one of the Lilleshall Company's managers. We used to go scrumping for pears in his garden, and if he ever caught us he gave us a good talking to! During the early 1920s I think the Lion Inn was run by a Mr Cliff. He was married to one of the daughters from Lee's Farm.

I mentioned Priorslee Hall Lodge. This was at the end of the long drive on the southern side of the Hall. The chauffeur lived there. His name was Ruscoe who also gave performances as the magician 'Professor Rockoe'. He was killed as he walked home from the Lion Inn one night. His brother took over the Lodge and became chauffeur to Mr Freeston.

Major Bishop lived in the big Red House at the back of the Lion and was by the entrance to where they used to keep visitors' cars for the Lion.

Jones' ran the wagonette service into Oakengates and Shifnal for shopping and I think they stored the carts near the row of houses now modernised and called Stable Row. Their horse may have been kept on a bit of ground not far from Tart's shop in Priorslee Road. There were some old railway lines close by Stable Row which went to the old Lawn Colliery.

The Woodhouse Pits were near the new Priors Lodge public house, on the eastern edge of the pools. We used to call one of the pools the 'Rough Raz', I don't know why we called it that. *(A probable explanation is that the field just south of the pool was once known as Rough Piece, so named on old tithe maps of the area.)*

My husband's brother Tom worked at Priorslee Furnaces. We used to watch the coke coming out of the big ovens when we were kids. I lived at Hollinswood for a while and had to pass them on the way to school. Hodson's had their Bone Mill at Hollinswood. It later became a Maggot Factory and moved to the side road opposite the Steel Rolling Mill at Sneds Hill.

I walked from Hollinswood, over the banks and came out by the Greyhound pub before going up Sneds Hill to the school. There was a coal pit on those banks *(Pudleyhill Colliery)* where the hole was covered only with some planks of wood. I used to drop stones down the shafts and wait until I could hear them splashing in the water at the bottom. I can remember there being an iron bucket full of coal halfway down the shaft.

There weren't really all that many houses in Priorslee when I was a girl. Just the ones in the village and the Square (the entrance was from a small road a few yards west of the Lion Inn) where there were quite a few houses. The main road to Shifnal divided the two. The Stafford Pits were reached by going down the Shifnal Road. Apparently there was once an old Toll Gate further on down that road, passed the Lodge but on the other side. You can't get down that road now because of the factories and the lake.

My friend and I used to go by the Woodhouse Pits and down Deakin's Lane (there was a big farm along there. I fancy it was Castle Farm owned by the Kelsalls.) until we came out on the Shifnal Road. The farm is underneath the lake now. You could go and help pick blackcurrants for a three ha'pence per pound weight.

My husband once took me to see Priorslee after all the new houses had been built. It broke my heart to see it, it really did.

George Leese

Dennis George Lees was born on 8th October 1931 at Wrockwardine Wood, and went to the 'Glassus' (Glasshouse) School. His father Ron was a miner at the Granville Colliery, Donnington. George first worked as a farm labourer at Belle Vue Farm run by the Chiltons in Wrockwardine Wood before he went to work for Thomas Tranter at Priorslee Hall Farm in 1948. He has lived in Priorslee ever since and is married to Doreen.

Mr Tom Tranter leased the Hall Farm from the Lilleshall Company, and after he died the farm was taken over by his son Ernie.

When I began work at the farm we still used horses for much of the heavy work, but tractors were just starting to be used. We did mixed farming; arable, dairy cattle, pigs, fowl and a few sheep later on after I arrived. Almost all the farms around here were the same as far as produce was concerned; they didn't concentrate on any one thing.

They all did a bit of everything. Wheat, potatoes, mixed corn, sugar beet, swedes, mangels, kale, all sorts. The Hall farm was 200 acres and when I came here we had seven workers: Mr Jones,

Clarence Addison, George Evans, two of the White's lads, Fred Palin, myself and, of course, Ernie and the gaffer. We had so many men because almost everything had to be done by hand.

I was paid 28s – £1.40p – a week in 1948; when I finished a few years ago it was about £70. Not a lot for the hours we had to do, but all farm labourers were paid about the same. I had to most things; milking, ploughing; anything to do with farming, I did it.

We used an old binder to cut corn. After it was cut we stood the stooks up to dry for about two weeks (depending on the weather), then it was brought into the barn and stacked. During the winter we thrashed it out, all by hand. We fed the cattle with the straw and also used it for bedding and for the fowl. Most of the grain was used for feeding the animals and fowl at that time, but Tranters used to sell some of the wheat. The potatoes and swedes were sold through Tranter's Wholesalers of St Georges. That was another side to their business.

The cattle were both dairy and beef; a lorry from Smith's, a haulage firm from Hadley, used to come to the farm every day and take the milk away in churns to Bridgnorth, I can't remember who had it to start with but the Midland Counties Dairy had it towards the end. The beef cattle were taken to the Smithfield at Wellington to be auctioned before slaughtering, and the sheep as well.

Talkng of sheep, I did do a little shearing but I was never very good at it, I couldn't do it properly. I made a mess of it; that's why we always had contractors in.

Farming was a lot slower in those days than it is today; the tractors weren't made to go fast then! Nowadays the machinery has got a lot bigger, can do a lot more things. And it's more dangerous. Another thing, they were only just starting to use fertilisers when I first came here, but not as much as they do now. The fertilisers were spread, often by hand and not by air like you can get these days. We also had to pick weeds out by hand, a back-breaking job, but by the early 60s the sprays had come out and we began using them. Much easier!

Priorslee Hall Farm's fields were all the way around the farm buildings, there weren't any separated or detached. We never had to go on the main road to reach a field, it was quite compact.

We didn't have a great deal to do with the other farms in the area until we started using combines, when we'd go and help down at the Castle Farm. The Kelsall's later took over one of the Woodhouse Farms, which had about 260 acres, and we used to help them because of their increased acreage. Castle Farm was just like ours, with mixed farming, and about the same size. Castle Farm's now underneath the lake at the end of Castle Farm Way.

I've always gone to both the Lion Inn and the Pigeon Box. Mr Heyward ran the Lion when I first came, followed by George Ramsden, Pat Shaw, Joe Storey and now Eddie Hickinbottom. All have been tenants of the brewery – the Wrekin Brewery at Wellington owned it. They were taken over by Wem Ales and then Greenall Whitley. Greenall's later bought out Davenports and introduced their beer into the Greenall pubs. To start with, the Lion was an Ind Coope house before Wrekin bought it in the 1930s.

Both pubs were just places to go and drink, have a natter, play in the dominoes and darts teams in the local leagues. You didn't have meals there then. I remember that they never sold many spirits at the Lion, mainly beer. The Lion had its own Cricket Club that played on a field down the Shifnal Road; there's a factory on it now. Millie Parry's husband used to play in the Cricket team.

The Lion had its own gardening club which finished some time ago, but I'm in the new one, called The Priorslee & District Horticultural Society, which was formed some 7 years ago and which has its show in the Priorslee Church Hall. The Lion Charity Show is held in the Lion and everything is auctioned off at night and the proceeds sent to the Orthopaedic Hospital at Oswestry.

I enter the vegetable and flower competitions which take place every September; I've got 5 cups at the moment from the 1991 competitions. Best Collection of Vegetables, Fuschias, Best Three Fuschias, Best in Show and second in the Best Kept Garden. They give 50-some-odd trophies out each year. Entries are restricted to members of the Club, and folk belong from all over. I'm a Life Member of the Club so I don't have to pay subs and more, but others pay something like £2 a year.

As with any pub that's been modernised, it's lost a lot of its character. There isn't any plastic in the Lion, it's all decent stuff, but it's somehow lost its character, but they have to make a living and attract the new locals and office workers in. They get a lot of office workers in there at lunch times for meals. In the old days you'd know everybody in the pub, but now you don't. Often you get strangers in and you don't know who they are.

They used to have annual trips, often for the men only, when they'd go off for the day somewhere. Usually Sundays. I've seen a photograph of Mrs Parry's husband on one. But that'd all stopped before I came here in the 50s.

The Pigeon Box has also been altered but it's still pretty much the same, but still a lot of strangers get in. Teagues' ran the pub when I first came, then Sergeant Howells, then his son Stan followed by Derek Kelly, Vic Parker, someone else and now Brian Money; Brian came up from Donnington. They still play darts and dominoes, but Stan Howells and Stan's two sons played cricket for the Lion. There was never any rivalry between the two pubs except that the darts and dominoes games were always needle matches. Davenports own the Pigeon Box as well as the Lion. Again, the Wrekin always owned the Pigeon Box until they were taken over, just like the Lion.

They used to slaughter cattle and pigs at the Pigeon Box, but I think that had finished by the time I came here.

The trade at both pubs doesn't seem to have been affected by the roads being cut off at the end, so I doubt they had much passing trade, just mainly locals.

Jack Jones ran the local bus service and kept his buses in a tin shed in Priorslee Village, where the first house on the right going into the village is now. I think they were old Bedford buses, but I could be wrong. They used to run every hour to St Georges, Oakengates and Wellington, and back. We used them to go shopping.

Terrington's store was a small shop down by the Pigeon Box that sold bread, groceries and general goods. I think the bread came from Willets' at Old Park. Harold Terrington and his wife Gladys also sold bacon and sausages, but not joints of meat. Mr Terrington was very friendly and would do anything for you. I believe the shop closed down during the middle 60s.

Apart from the Post Office I can't remember any other shops in Priorslee after I came. The Post Office was run from a little room at

J. JONES & Sons,
Priory Motor Services

●

Tours - Excursions
Contracts - Service

●

ANYWHERE—ANY TIME
ANY DISTANCE

●

No. 2 PRIORS LEE,
OAKENGATES, Salop.

FRIDAYS ONLY.
DEPARTURE TIMES ONLY.

	p.m.	p.m.	p.m.	p.m.	p.m.
Priors Lee	5.50	7-5	7-35	8-5	8-35
	9-20				

	p.m.	p.m.	p.m.	p.m.	p.m.
Oakengates	6-0	6-30	7-0	7:35	7-30
	7-45	8-0	8-15	8-30	9-5
	9-35	10-5			

	p.m.	p.m.	p.m.	p.m.	p.m.
St. Georges	6-5	6-40	7-10	7-20	7-40
	7-50	8-10	8-20	8-40	9-15
	9-45	10-15*			

* Priors Lee only.

Friday Service to be operated on Thursday before Good Friday except 8-15 p.m. from Oakengates.

SATURDAYS ONLY.

OAKENGATES & SHERIFFHALES.

			p.m.	p.m.
Oakengates	...	(Dep.)	4-30	8-35
St. Georges	...	(Dep.)	4-40	8-45

			p.m.	p.m.
Sheriffhales	...	(Dep.)	5-0	9-10
St. Georges	...	(Dep.)	—	9-20

Owners will make every effort to maintain all times stated, but will not be responsible for loss of connections through unforeseen circumstances.

FARES.

	Sgle.	Ret.
Priors Lee to Oakengates ...	3d.	5d.
St. Georges to Oakengates ...	2d.	3d.
Oakengates to Sheriffhales		1/-

Above and left:

Extracts from J Jones & Sons passenger timetables

the front of the house next door to the Lion, and it had a two-part stable door at the front. As well as stamps and the like they sold a few tins of food and home-made cakes. Mrs Biddulph kept it. There was a pillar box just outside, been there for many years until it was changed to a smaller box further up the road away from the house so that nobody would look straight through the window into the house after it finished being a Post Office during the late 70s.

The Square was just up from the Lion, on the same side before Dark Lane; it was called that because the houses were laid out in a square shape. Ron Withington who worked at the steel rolling mill lived in one of them, at the back. They've knocked all of them down now, I can't remember when. I'm hopeless with dates! The Lilleshall Company owned them and I think they were originally built as miners' cottages, same as some of the houses in the village on the other side of the Shifnal Road. There was also a farmhouse by Dark Lane that belonged to Sid Lee.

The village didn't change much in appearance until after Telford Development Corporation started. One row was extensively altered, and I think that Stable Row was knocked down and completely rebuilt with the original bricks. They tried to alter it but the mortar was so bad that they couldn't do anything with it.

All the pits had been closed for a long time before I came to Priorslee, but there were spoil heaps and tips everywhere that wasn't farmland. My wife used to swim in the Rough Pool, and got changed in some small changing rooms that were on where the little island in the lake is now.

That island was then part of the causeway between the main Flash or Hangie's Pool and the Rough, with the mineral railway line not far off. Years ago water from the Rough was pumped down to the steel rolling mill, like they did from the Lawn Pit. Dirty, yellowish water pumped from the disused Woodhouse Pit went into a third pool, the Oily, before it went into Wesley Brook. Wesley Brook now runs into the Balancing Lake at the Castle Farm Interchange before going on towards Shifnal and joining the River Wharf on its way to the River Severn at Bridgnorth.

Freeston's lived at the Hall when I came, then Willis Brown, Oxleys, then Bruce Ball before the Corporation took it over. Mrs Parry knows more about that than I do. Where the offices on the western side are now used to be gardens and greenhouses together with a pool and a little boat-house. The offices are roughly where the pool was.

It must be about 20 years ago that the Corporation started levelling out the mounds, building the new roads ready for all the new housing estates at Priorslee. All the buildings at the Lawn Pit, which was on the other side of the bank opposite the Lion, together with those at the Stafford Pit (on what is now part of Stafford Park) were demolished as well. The Woodhouse Colliery banks were shifted before the Bovis houses were built there. Some of the pit banks had been on fire with internal combustion! In fact, some of the Woodhouse banks were lugged away for airfield construction during the War.

Before the offices were built we never used to see any traffic at all except for the bloke that came to fetch the milk from our farm and the occasional visitor. Mr Parry, chauffeur at the Hall, came every morning to get milk for the offices. The road then only came down to the Hall and the Farm; it wasn't a through road.

It's totally different now!

Millie Parry

Millie Parry (née Dean) was born in Friesland Cottages, St Georges on 20th September 1901, and is Priorslee's oldest resident. After leaving school at 16 she took up tailoring for Edwin Ball at Oakengates' Market Street until she married Belcher 'Bel' Parry in 1930. Thereafter she did occasional work for Mr Ball as well as Dickens of Oakengates. Bel became chauffeur for the Lilleshall Company at Priorslee Hall. After her husband died in 1957 Millie was employed as cook and housekeeper for Mrs Bruce Ball who occupied the Hall at the time. When Telford Development Corporation purchased the Hall, Millie was retained to make coffee, tea, etc., for the Board members. She retired in 1977 and still lives in one of the Hall Farm cottages.

I recall there being one little shop – Butlers – in the old Sneds Hill, on the right hand side of the road leading from the Four Ways towards St Georges. They had the shop in their front room and you could get pop, sweets, all sorts of little odds and ends, and household essentials. They did quite a good trade really.

Mr Tart the policeman ran a shop, owned by Bannisters, down by the Pigeon Box. Two houses have been built on the land where it was. They sold mostly groceries, cheese and bacon; it was a very nice little shop. The only other shop in Priorslee was Biddulph's on the Shifnal Road; they sold mostly sweets. It became the Post Office, but an older Post Office used to be higher up on the corner at one time. Biddulph's son had a house built in the garden behind the shop. It's still there.

Mr Howells who ran the Pigeon Box used to play cricket with my husband for the Lion Inn's team. Both pubs haven't changed a great deal on the outside, but they've both been modernised on the inside. From what I hear, they're quite go-ahead young people who have them now.

Stone House, on the left of the Lion Inn, used to belong to the Lilleshall Company. Mr Kenworthy, one of the officials of the company, lived there. Champion Jones lived at Ivy Grove just in the Village; I think he had something to do with the Pits. They, like all the Lilleshall Company houses, have since been sold.

The Lilleshall Company owned practically everything in Priorslee and Sneds Hill; the pits, the farms, the houses, even the School and the Church.

The old Village was a bit dilapidated, old fashioned. Not much money was either available or spent on maintenance, so it all got a bit run down. But the Corporation took it down to square one and renovated a lot of it. Made really good houses out of what was there before. Much nicer now. The houses now called Stable Row were remodelled from the original bricks; they made them beautiful! Some friends of mine lived in one, and it was beautiful, with a lovely garden as well.

The whole area around the Village was covered in pit mounds, very ugly. And the pools: one used to grow and grow when more water went into it. There was the Rough, where my brothers went swimming as boys, and the overflow into the bigger pool that seemed to creep towards St Georges! They sometimes mentioned a pool called the 'Spring', but I don't know where that was, I never found out.

Even the house that's now the doctor's surgery was one of the Lilleshall houses. Joe Teague and his family lived there when I was a wee girl. I don't know what he did exactly, but he must have had a good job in the Offices to get a house like that. I used to go there every day and get a big tin of milk for a few coppers. I don't think they'd sell it as a regular thing, but as a boy my elder brother was always keen on gardening and worked there. That's how we got to know them. They gave us apples and all sorts of things out of the garden. Hail, rain or sunshine, we had milk from there. It wasn't a farm, though; perhaps they kept one cow and this was surplus that they let us have.

As for bus services! It's disgraceful what we've had to put up with since the local bus services were 'rationalised' over ten years ago. We don't really have much of a bus service now. I have to wait for someone to take me shopping in their car. Unless you've got your own car, things are difficult. Ernie Tranter, the farmer, always used to take me shopping, he was as good as gold!

In the old days we used Jack Jones' bus service. He had a heart of gold. He'd do anything for you. When we used to go to the Priorslee Hall Lodge, where my husband and I lived when he was the Company chauffeur, the bus should have terminated in the Village but Jack would shout down the bus, 'Sit thee down, lass, I'll take thee home!' He kept his bus in the Village, and it saved me having to walk down the road passed the Lion, especially if it was a bad night.

I remember there was a girl once who was crying because she'd missed the last bus to Sherrifhales. Again, Jack said,'Sit thee down. I'll see's that you get home!' And he took her all the way home for nothing! He was very kind, good hearted and a bit of a character.

The school at Priorslee was built by the Lilleshall Company last century for the children of all the folk who worked for the company in the area. We were very fond of the teachers. Mr Upton, the Headmaster, was bent double, nearly in two, I don't know what his problem was, perhaps something wrong with his spine. But he was a good man. Mr Price and Mrs Turner were teachers; she was a lovely person. I can remember her giving us lessons on Home Management, and I was thrilled to bits! That made up my mind. I wasn't going to carry on doing things the way I at home, and I

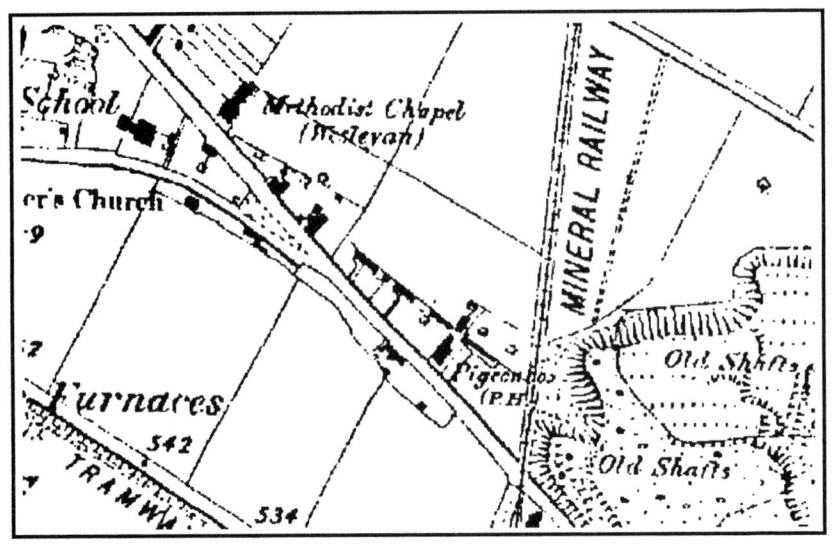

Location of Priorslee School and Pigeon Box Inn

Priorslee School, c. 1900

couldn't wait to get home quick enough to do my jobs the way she said!

We also had to go to Sunday School at St Peter's Church. At one time we used to go to the Methodist Chapel on Priorslee Road, but I don't remember when or why we started going to St Peter's. Several of us went, including Mrs Margerrison when she was a girl with me, and I used to sing something soft or silly during the hymns, which made them all laugh! I didn't think I'd been spotted, but I did get told off and ordered to go home! Oh, I was upset about it! I told my mother that I was never going back again, but she said, 'Oh, yes, you are!' And I did, but I cried and cried. So I went back and some of the elder girls made a fuss of me and everything was all right.

We went on several Sunday School trips when I was a wee girl. I think we went with the Mount Zion Chapel on top of the hill. That's been down many, many years. It was falling apart even then, because of Pit subsidence. My grandmother used to sing and recite there as a girl. On Sunday School outings we'd go in Tranter's farm brakes – big, open wagons with seats either side – to places like Cherrington and Ellerdine, and we thought it was wonderful! We'd have a picnic and play games in the fields and pick apples from the trees. We really looked forward to them!

I had the time of my life in the Church Institute! We had dances every weekend put on by Mr Griffiths who looked after it. I seem to remember it was a big tin place, made of corrugated iron sheets. It had a very big room. Mrs McLoughlin taught us how to waltz and other dances. Square dances, quadrilles, the Lancers. I can't tell you how much I enjoyed them! Lots of people went there, including my brothers and sisters.

I don't remember there being many sports there at that time except those put on by the Church. We did have egg-and-spoon racing and things like that for the younger children.

The farms used to belong, like everything else, to the Lilleshall Company. There was no electric or gas in the Village early on, and folk had candles and oil lamps in their homes.

As children we often went down to the Brook near Kelsall's Castle Farm. There was a small sandy place down there, and it was just like being at the sea-side! We'd take something to eat and milk from the farm. There was an old Dutch lady, complete with clogs, who worked at Castle Farm. She was a funny old thing! The Kelsall's were Quakers, a very nice family. We very seldom went to any of the other farms.

My father William worked as a miner at the Woodhouse Pit and we often went for walks there. I never had a head for heights, but we used to walk up the steps made from big planks, like railway sleepers, and at the top you could see through the planks into the shaft below. My stomach used to turn over!

Father worked hard and died young, only 59 years old. He had gases on his stomach; when he breathed heavily when resting at home you could smell the gas coming off his chest. He also had heart and kidney trouble brought on by working in the Pit. He was a poor old man at 59. Health and safety in the mines wasn't what it is now.

The Stafford Pit, opposite the Lodge and on the southern side of the Shifnal Road, was only kept open to extract the water and prevent it from flooding the other pits in the area. I think the Lawn Pit was closed for working but the water was also pumped from there for the same reason but used in the rolling mill at Sneds Hill. I believe mining at the Stafford and Lawn Pits had finished before I came along, but the Woodhouse Pit continued working until much later.

My husband and I lived at the Lodge after we were married. He was the chauffeur to the Company, a very responsible job. We lived there until the 1940s when we moved into the Hall Farm cottages. He always drove good class cars, I can't remember their makes, and took the old Earl of Granville all over the place. The young Earl liked to drive the car himself. My husband drove all the important people, picked them up from and returned them to the railway station. He did ordinary jobs as well, like fetching the wages if he was available, and could converse with people from all walks of life. Cyril Nicholls, the Company Secretary, said he was more essential to the Company than most. Indispensible.

My husband was a real gentleman. Always looked smart in his uniform – navy blue suit with chauffeur's cap – and was very well mannered. 'Tall, smart and handsome,' as my mother used to say. The suit was tailored by Steventon's at Wellington.

Priorslee Hall, c. 1930

My husband used to go and shoot pheasants and hares during the harvest time when all the activity startled them. I do miss the hares! Sometimes I'd say, 'I don't know what we're going to have for dinner tomorrow.' And he'd take himself off into the fields and come back with something. He wasn't supposed to have the pheasants (they were strictly for folk at the Hall), but we often did! I remember that one day I saw partridges in the garden just as my husband was returning from Shifnal after fetching the wages. I pointed them out to him; he fetched his gun and we finished up eating them. He was a good shot!

He was also a good cricketer, especially bowler but also an all-rounder, deputy captain of the Lion Cricket Club (the vicar was the captain). They played many a match to win cups and trophies. The pitch was just opposite the Lodge, so he didn't have far to go!

Quite a number of things took place at the Hall, not only business. For example, at Christmas time a band used to come inside and play.

We actually lived inside the Hall for some of the War years. All the girls except the cook were taken off to help the War effort. The cook lived in the Village and went home at night to her husband, so the old people in the Hall were left on their own. They didn't like it, so they asked my husband, his mother (who lived with us at the time) and I to move in for the duration. In fact, the only reason we left there was because they were going to put someone else in the Lodge.

But I didn't really want to go; I'd got used to living in the Hall and was quite happy there. Who wouldn't be? And then I was back cooking on top of a very small stove again, it was a nuisance! Especially when I came to make jam and marmalade, it just wasn't designed to make life easy! My mother-in-law said not to bother, but we had to have both jam and marmalade.

The kitchen in the Hall during Bruce Ball's time was nice and big. Everything was refurbished with beautiful furniture all round, cupboards to match with double sinks and a large AGA cooker as well as an electric stove and a mixer. Plenty of room and work surfaces. The floor was covered in red Marley tiles. I enjoyed cleaning them with soapy water and a drop or two of paraffin oil at weekends: it gave such a polish! It looked lovely! I was so proud of that kitchen, it was a joy to work in.

When we got married Mr Freeston lived at the Hall and Bruce Ball came later. I can remember my mother telling me that a Mr McKinley lived there before the Freestons. There was also Willis Brown, but he didn't reign long; I don't know what he did, but whatever it was meant that he didn't stay in residence for very long. The Browns and Freestons were very good friends, came from Sheffield, and stayed at the Hall quite frequently as guests of the Freestons.

Mr Oxley, another Managing Director of the Company, also lived at the Hall for a while, a bit before the War if I remember rightly. He was very good at his job, although he was fond of his tipple. The dividends picked up and the Company was even able to issue extra shares free to existing shareholders during his time. Mrs Oxley was a very nice person who died of cancer after a breast operation. Very sad. I seem to remember that one of her daughters never gave her a bit of peace.

The gardens at the Hall were very pretty. I often picked the fruit when they gave me permission. Raspberries, blackcurrants and gooseberries in particular. Mrs Freeston used to say, 'Parry, never go short on vegetables! If you haven't got any there's always plenty in the Hall!' Of course, we weren't on big wages but it was always regular, and these little extras were of great benefit. They were very kind to us.

The Lilleshall Company Engineering Department was closed down during the Slump in Mr Freeston's time. Things were very bad then. Doris Tranter's father had worked there as a boy and went back to work for the Company when things picked up, but he said it was pitiful to see it, it was not a patch on what it had been before.

Years before, the Lilleshall Company had such a wonderful reputation that men went all over the world erecting things for the company. It never really regained its former glory after the Slump, and has steadily declined over the years. Things, as I said, picked up in Oxley's time, but never to the same extent. What was left of the Lilleshall Company became a new company, Lilleshall Plc. We are now getting better dividends than we did from the old company. I think they're based in Bristol now. It's sad when you think they once employed, housed, educated and entertained so many people in the area, not just Priorslee.

After the Corporation bought the Hall I was kept on to make coffee and suchlike for the Board. They were very good to me and I don't think I'd ever been invited to so many parties in my life!

The Village was once a very quiet place; my sister used to say, 'You want to get somewhere where it's civilised!'

It's very different now!

Billy Pascall

William 'Billy' H Pascall was born at Grove Street, St Georges on 21st December 1914 and attended St Georges Church of England School. His father, also named William, was killed in an explosion at the Woodhouse Pit in 1932. Billy up bricklaying at the age of 15 and travelled throughout the country doing civil engineering work before enlisting in the army in 1942. He was demobbed as Class B in 1945, married Vera and lived at Cannock before moving back to the Priorslee area. He then went to work at Sankey's and retired as a foreman in the civil engineering section in 1978.

There wasn't very much to do in Priorslee when we were children. This was a very depressed area in the 1920s and 1930s and wages were very low. Some said that the Lilleshall Company robbed the poor to pay the rich. They never seemed to invest anything in the people; the shareholders wanted as much as they could get.

There were, of course, some social evenings, but there was a strict discipline imposed by our parents; we had to be back home by 9 o'clock. Many of the social events took place in the chapels. I was a member of the gymnastics clubs at St Georges and Donnington and went three times a week. The gym classes taught us how to wield India clubs, perform statues and hand springs, boxing – in fact anything to do with gymnastics.

I very seldom went to the concerts; children had to go with a grown-up, but there were occasions when an hour-long social event was laid on just for the youngsters, starting at either 6 or 7 o'clock, and you had to get home quickly afterwards. We played Postman's Knock and Blind Man's Buff together with a bit of dancing to old gramophone records and had food if we took some with us. There wasn't much food to spare then, we were rationed. We paid a penny to go towards the lighting and heating.

I remember that the Institute had a billiard room and a football team – in fact, my brother Geoff used to play for Priorslee. There are some of the old Priorslee footballers still about. I can't remember when the team disbanded, sometime during the 1940s, I think. Some rare things took place in the Institute – lads riding bicycles inside. One chap in particular rode his bicycle on top of a billiard table without falling off!

Many social events took place there in the 1930s – whist drives, Mothers' Union meetings, rummage sales and so on. I think the Church helped to provide funds for it.

My family lived at Rock Terrace in St Georges before moving to Freeston Avenue in Priorslee. I've attended St Georges Church, Sneds Hill Chapel and St Peter's Church, Priorslee. I went to the Mission Church, the Granville Mission, Muxton Mission, all of them in turn.

I was in the Church of England Scouts at St Georges and later formed my own troop of Scouts and Cubs with Tommy Dawes at Snedshill Chapel in Priorslee. Even though it was based at the Chapel it was 'free', not attached to any particular denomination. It was because of it being open to anyone that we had quite a rough crowd of colliers' children who could only afford a penny or a ha'penny each week to attend.

When they bought their uniforms they would have to buy one item every month, perhaps starting with a neckerchief or pair of socks and then a pair of shorts when the socks had been paid for, and so on. By the time they'd paid for the shorts the socks would be worn out! Of course, some parents could afford to pay for jerseys as well, but most were quite badly off. Nevertheless, each boy had got at least one part of the uniform. Our colours were green with a yellow neckerchief. They were damn good lads!

Our troop won trophies for every competition we entered, such as football and field craft. I never had a minute to spare; I used to come back from work and go out straight away to organise a paper chase or something else. We taught them the Scout Laws, how to tie different knots, how to survive, how to track by recognising all the animal spoors, collect wild flowers (and name them!) and so on. In fact, there wasn't a wild flower around here that you could name and I didn't know where it was to be found! I knew every footpath around here.

At weekends we used to go out on the banks (pit mounds), pitch a tent and let the cubs sleep away from home overnight until they went back on the Sunday. The children cooked their own food (under our supervision) and had a great time!

When I was in the Scouts, about a dozen of us used to go, bugles sounding, to a different church or chapel every Sunday night. We even went to the Salvation Army. Not only churches in Priorslee, St Georges, Sneds Hill, Muxton and Donnington but also to Oakengates, Dawley, in fact any of them that would have us. It was good, because we'd always got a bit of backing through not being tied to a single place. They all donated towards tents and other things. There was some method in it, but we all used to enjoy it.

We'd decide where we were going and write them a letter to let them know, and the churchfolk would all be waiting for us, shaking hands and so on. All told we had between 20 and 30 regular members, but not all were able to come all the time.

We went swimming in the 'Rough Razzer' (Hangman's Pool or The Flash). There were three pools; The Flash, The 'Oily' and the man-made Reservoir. We changed on the side of the pool; no swimming trunks, just a big handkerchief or a pair of football shorts! We weren't proud, there wasn't any money to spend on luxuries.

The Lilleshall Company's mineral railway line came down from the Woodhouse Pits, passed the Oily Pool, along Hangman's Hill

Priorslee Post Office

Demolition of the chimney stack at the Woodhouse Pit

and down what is now part of the main road from Telford's Mark roundabout on the A5 to the main Priorslee roundabout by the Shifnal Road. The Woodhouse Pits were near Dixon's Farm – the Woodhouse Farm. The farmhouse is still there, a red house standing on its own with new estate houses surrounding it.

The Doctor's Surgery next to the present newsagents' shop was lived in by Mrs Tranter and her daughter Lillian after Mr Tranter died and they had to leave his farm, and later by her son Paul before it became the Surgery. A foreman or manager (Mr Beech?) of something to do with the Lilleshall Company (possibly the Steel Mill) lived in the house before the Tranters.

During the 1926 General Strike (and at other times) I used to help dig out coal from makeshift pits when the proper Pits were boycotted. In fact, I lost one of my schoolfriends who sat next to me when he got buried down by The Rookery banks between St Georges and Donnington.

I sometimes went with my grandparents to the Muxtonbridge mine at Donnington as well as on the banks near Hangman's Hill. My grandparents had a horse and trap to carry the sacks on. When the horse went lame my father got into the shafts and pulled the trap himself. He almost got killed one time; he had about a ton of coal on board when he very nearly lost control going down a hill, but he didn't let go of the shafts. It was marvellous to see his strength prevent a serious accident as the trap gained speed!

There were several pit ponies here; Harry Price was the ostler at the Woodhouse Pit. Gordon Anslow's grandfather was ostler at the Grange Pit. Both were little men. Isaac Smith was another one. They had the best remedies out for all ills, including broken limbs – horse liniment! I still believe in it and I still get some, even now! It stinks, but it's lovely stuff!

When the ponies retired from the pits they were turned out on the Rough (the field south of Hangman's Hill). Even though they were totally blind, their blinkers were left on. They could still recognise the voices of the men who had driven them down the pit, and sidled over to them and were fed apples and scraps of food. It was rather touching.

Gordon Anslow and his father 'Laddie' Anslow killed pigs. He was a farm labourer who may once have worked in the Pits and left them because of ill health. He went to Dixon's Farm and later left to work at Lee's Farm on Dark Lane. Then he left Lee's and went back to Dixon's, then run by Frank Dixon. Alf Dixon runs another farm on the Red Hill.

Nearly every cottager in the old days kept chickens in a pen and pigs in a small pigsty. There's nothing like having your own eggs! But as soon as a chicken went broody and stopped laying, its time was up, and you'd get another to replace it! There weren't any restrictions on keeping pigs. You'd kill a pig when you had to. Everything was used, the intestines, the bacon, the pork, nothing was lost, only the squeal!

Gordon travelled from house to house, charging about three shillings to kill each pig, hang it and go back to cut it up, salt the flitches and hams on the settlice with saltpetre on the bone so that the bone didn't rot. And a woman was never allowed to touch a pig before it was about to be cooked, especially if she was on her monthlies! It was taboo. The pig would go bad if touched by a woman, that was the belief. If ever you saw a woman in a butcher's shop she was only allowed to wrap the pork up, never touch it! Wrap it up, put it in the basket and take the money. Nothing else.

There were very few shops in Priorslee or Sneds Hill. There was one, a sweet and grocery store which also sold odds and ends (darning wool and other essentials), on Stafford Road where Sneds Hill 'Four Ways' is, next to four old cottages (now demolished). There was another shop in Freeston Avenue (run by Mrs Nock), then Mrs Barrister had a general grocery near the Pigeon Box on the other side of the road. The Post Office was run by Mrs Biddulph down by the Lion Inn. She sold tobacco, cigarettes, sweets as well as stamps, and would also order foodstuffs if anyone wanted them.

There were more shops (including about six butchers!) in St Georges and most people tended to go there, or Oakengates. You have to remember that Sneds Hill and Priorslee were little more than small settlements, nothing like a town. I can remember Freeston Avenue being built, and all the housing which covers the area now. It just wasn't there when I was a lad! Everything was open land, fields and spoil heaps.

Sneds Hill Square was at the crossroads above the Pigeon Box, and the Coal Wharf was just below the Box. Sergeant Howells lived in a little row of cottages by the mineral line to the Woodhouse Pit. Priorslee Road then continued straight into the village and went off to the left towards the Lawn Pit, long before the roundabout was built in the 1970s or 1980s. The mineral line crossed the road where the island is now and there was a level crossing gate there to hold up traffic when the engines needed to pass through.

Wooden troughs were supported on scaffolding about 16 feet high across the Shifnal road, and they carried water bucket-pumped from the Lawn Pit all the way down to a reservoir above the steel rolling mill on Sneds Hill. I can remember the furnaces there very well, because when they opened the coke ovens it was like a red sky at night for hours on end while the coke was being knocked out of the ovens, especially when the top of the cupola was open and flames shot into the air. The smell was awful! Very sulphury!

Priorslee Square was behind the Lion Inn. A lot of people lived up there, and the main road divided the Square from the Village. They were very clannish, and if you borrowed something from anyone it had to be returned, even a jug of beer! (They brewed beer in the Square.) It was really like two settlements, not one. Although people brewed their own beer, the pub survived because folk went there for a natter and to swap yarns, and you can't take your own beer into a pub!

The Lion was once a coach house, in a different community to those that went to the Pigeon Box. Unless one of the pubs ran out of beer, everyone went to their own inn. The Pigeon Box had a slaughter house at the back for killing pigs and cattle. Gordon Anslow went there as well as to peoples' houses to do his work. They've still got the hanging hooks in the ceiling above the bar. Pigeon racing has always been very popular around here and that's probably why the pub is called the Pigeon Box, but I'm not sure. The mill workers would go to the nearest pub to set the pigeons off, and the Pigeon Box was the closest after the works canteen.

The pub was also used to share out money when the men got paid at the Pit. You see, there were four men in what was called a Stall, or a gang, and they pooled all their wages according to what they'd done in the mine. Diggers got more than packers (who shovelled the coal into boxes), and the money was divided equally between the members of the Stall. I know I got paid more money working at Sankey's than my father got for working down the Pit, and he worked longer hours than I did.

Castle Farm was run by the Kelsall family. They were Quakers. My brother Albert worked there as a cowman. There was once an Iron Age and Roman settlement there; that's probably why it's called Castle Farm.

Kelsall's children were Johnny, Buck, Bill and Mary. They all helped on the farm and never turned anyone away. If you worked there you had your breakfast and tea provided; at harvest time they'd come round with a basket of victuals and a jug of cider or beer. At the farm, everyone was fed at the same table. They were the world's best employers.

As a lad I used to go potato picking in the fields, cocked the sheaves of corn (there weren't any combines then), eight sheaves stooked up with one on the top to hold them down. Then the threshing machine separated the stalks from the grain. We got covered in dust, black as the ace of spades! The chaff was used as deep litter for poultry; the chickens scratched around for missed grain. I also gathered hay with a long wooden rake, scooping it into piles. Balers were just appearing, but Kelsalls didn't have one then.

When I came out of the army and wandered about the fields, perhaps picking water cress from Wesley Brook, Mr Kelsall would see that it was me and let me carry on, but if it was anybody else, a stranger, he'd be after them! I always shut the gates after me, mended fences or helped to bring stray cattle in.

I can remember once, when I was cutting some holly in the dark on a Christmas Eve, I was up the top of the tree where the berries were bigger and better. Young Buck turned up and shouted out, "Hey, you! What're you doing up there?"

I called down, "Just wait a minute, sonny, while I come down."

Remember, I'd just come out of the army, and I said, "Now, sonny, you run home and tell your father that I fought for this country and I'm going to live on it!" Just like that.

The next Sunday morning I was with my brother Albert and Buck said to him, "That's the fella! But don't you say nothing to him!"

Albert told him I was his brother and that I'd eat him alive if he said anything!

Mind you, I never did any harm really. I just took the odd vegetable, perhaps a swede, if I needed one. Never more than I needed. I also did a bit of rabbiting and ferreting. My father kept ferrets. I put wire snares down for the rabbits and had a 404 rifle, but never went on anybody's land with it unless I had permission.

We used to have a stewpot on the old-fashioned hob, and it was never empty! While one rabbit was in there another would be waiting! The pot only got cleaned out on a Friday night. We had a mug and some pearl barley next to the pot, and Friday night was senna tea night. I hated it! And if you had a bit of a spot on you, it was a mug of infused pearl barley to cure it, or, if you had a cough, some butter and sugar on a spoon together with a mouthful of sulphur.

There were lots of rabbits, foxes and badgers here when I was a boy. Now there's only a few foxes and rabbits left. I remember dogs catching badgers, and we used to dig fox cubs out on the Castle Farm land by the brook. There was a publican at Hinstock who took them from us, or we sent them to the Hunt at Albrighton. They kept them for training the hounds to follow the scent. Mind you, if we dug out a fox or vixen, you could say it had had it.

But we never killed for killing's sake. I always liked to see the foxes, especially in the sunlight stalking along a hedge. It's the most wonderful sight I've ever seen. The colour of the red fur is lovely!

Frank Dixon

Frank Dixon was born at Allscott near Wellington on 8th June 1917. His father, also named Frank, ran a farm there until moving to Admaston in 1926 and working at the Sugar Beet Factory at Allscott. From 1930 the family farmed at Condover near Shrewsbury and in 1936 took over the tenancy of Lower Woodhouse Farm, Priorslee. After his father died in 1947, Frank managed the farm for his mother Lucy and eventually went into partnership with her. From 1962 to 1970 he farmed the land with his wife Maisie until Telford Development Corporation purchased it, after which he worked for the Telford Trust. He retired in 1982 but continued to live in the farmhouse until 1986.

None of the farms in Priorslee were owned privately; they were all rented from the Lilleshall Company who in turn leased them from Lord Stafford who actually owned both the farms and the land.

There were four farms called 'Woodhouse Farm', three of them in Priorslee. The one where I lived, Lower Woodhouse Farm, was by the Woodhouse Pit. The proper Woodhouse Farm is to the east of my farm and is currently managed by John Harmer. On the top of the Red Hill, where my nephew lives now, was the Upper Woodhouse Farm, and on the Donnington side of the A5 was another Woodhouse Farm. All were known as 'The Woodhouse', which was a little confusing.

There were three other farms in the area: Dark Lane Farm run by the Lee brothers; Castle Farm by the Kelsalls, and Priorslee Hall Farm run by Tom Tranter and later his son Ernie.

The sizes of the farms were as follows: mine was about 115 acres; the Upper Woodhouse some 130 acres and the Woodhouse about 200 acres; Kelsall's Farm (Castle Farm) 250 acres; Tranter's Farm was about 200 acres; and Lee's Farm around 300 acres.

We did mixed farming at the Lower Woodhouse, but dairy cattle were the most important and biggest side. We grew a few cereals, sugar beet and potatoes. We didn't keep sheep after the first couple of years I farmed there because we had too much trouble with dogs worrying them. Nor did we do much beef in those days. We did have a few pigs and chickens, of course. About two or three hundred chickens, not a lot. We never really went into poultry in a big way. We sold a few eggs to the Egg Marketing Board, who came and fetched them once a fortnight, about 90 dozen. We also sold a few at the door. Some folk came for them every Sunday for almost 40 years! They very seldom missed.

There was a part of the Wesley Brook which had bricks built on either side with a narrow entrance at one end. Bits of it are still there. A big iron plate was slotted between the bricks and into the stream to dam it up, about four or five foot deep, and the sheep were pushed into the water to wash the wool free of flies and maggots before shearing. No chemicals were used. The water from the pools by the Woodhouse Pit fed the stream, but they could divert water pumped from the old Lawn Pit if there was a shortage. This didn't happen very often because the water from the Lawn was discoloured.

Normally we'd kill only two pigs a year, just for the house during the war. Everything was on ration, terrible really, and two pigs would keep us in bacon for the full twelve months. A chap named Harry Anslow came to kill and prepare them. He's dead now, poor chap. 'round Christmas he'd be very busy slaughtering in the area. He worked for us, actually, for quite a number of years. He was very handy. Never killed anything on a Sunday.

Lower Woodhouse Farm

After he'd cut them up I'd do the salting – dry salting – down in the cellar. We bought big blocks of salt, about 14 pounds in a block. I remember my mother never let any female touch a pig, I don't know why, but she was really brilliant at making anything like sausage, black pudding, pork pies; nothing was wasted, nothing. You'd never tasted anything like it in your life!

We used to milk about 35 or 40 cattle and grew sugar beet on about 10 acres, 8 or 9 acres of potatoes. During the War we were more or less told what to grow by the Ministry of Agriculture and which fields we'd have to plough up. Even if a field had been pasture for many years you couldn't get out of doing what they said. They even controlled the prices of the milk and cereals.

The Ministry of Food told us where to send all the potatoes and wheat grain we produced but we were allowed to keep oats and barley for our own use, and all the cattle. For instance, we might be told to send 10 tons of potatoes down the the Rhondda Valley. I must have put hundreds of tons on the trains at Oakengates and Shifnal Stations, to go all over the country. Hundreds of tons, all in hundredweight sacks. I took them down on a trailer, three tons at a time. They could load up to nine tons in a railway truck.

The milk from the cattle went to the Midland Counties Dairy at Penn, near Wolverhampton. That was very little trouble, really. We used to get a few complaints at times, to do with butter fat and solids in the milk, but we always came out right.

A firm called Clark & Smith's collected the milk in lorries, once a day at about 8 o'clock in the morning. All the milk was in churns. They did nothing else but collect milk from farms unless they took sugar beet during the annual campaign down to the Beet Factory at Allscott. In those days almost every wagon going down the Shifnal Road towards Wolverhampton and Birmingham belonged to Clark & Smith's. Later the same day you'd see them all coming back again, fleets of them.

Until 1944, when we bought a milking machine, all the milking was done by hand. It made milking so much easier, and quicker. During summertime in the War, though, I used to milk in the morning at about 6 o'clock. After that I'd drive the tractor until 10 or 12 o'clock at night. My fields were grouped very much together. All the arable was from where the Telford's Mark island is on the A5 right across down to the lane that goes to Shifnal. There were four biggish fields on one side of the road (from about $12\frac{1}{2}$ to 18 acres apiece), all ploughed. There was another little field at the top of the lane (it's been made into a coppice, planted with trees) that we ploughed as well. The field where Barratt Homes built all their houses was also ploughed.

When I started at the farm I only had a tractor, an old 1939 Ford. In 1940/41 we had a brand new Ford tractor delivered and it cost £177. Modern tractors cost something like £24,000! It's unbelievable!

To start with, the corn crops were cut with a binder, then stooked, carted off, stacked and then thrashed, all by hand. Very hard work. And you'd have to carry the two-hundredweight bags on your back about 50 yards from the old barn to the granary. Farming in the early days was hard work, but fun. We used to enjoy it. I don't really know what was enjoyable about it, but we were young and that makes the difference. The pace of life was quite slow, no desparate hurry, but you'd have to work and stick at it. You wouldn't rush at a job.

In the harvest, you'd never seen anything like it, in the War. The men would come out of the Pit, wash their faces in the horse trough, and they'd be helping us harvest until 5 or 6 o'clock at night. They wouldn't accept any wages, they wouldn't be paid, all they had was barrels of cider – as much as they wanted – and 'harvest rations' – bread and cheese. I've seen as many as 28 men in the Woodhouse at night. The most men we employed full time was three, so you can see that at harvest time we made good use of help from the miners.

We also used to have Harvest Suppers at the Farm in October/November, and cook a goose for the men who'd helped. They enjoyed it! But no, they'd never get paid; they wouldn't accept it and got annoyed if you offered them money. My dad was a very generous man. He enjoyed a pint, and used to go across to the pub, the Quarry opposite St Georges Church, and treat them to a drink or two. He was very popular, my dad was!

Apart from casual labour to pull beet or pick potatoes, during the war we had prisoners of war, Italians first (they weren't much good) and later Germans, from the camps at Sherrifhales. They were dropped off in lorries or buses in the morning and were picked up again at 5 o'clock at night. They had exactly the same food as we had. When they first came they only had a lump of bread and two links of sausage to last them through the day, so mother had them in to eat the same as us. Chicken, beef, whatever we had, they had, and they appreciated it.

The language problem wasn't very good, but we managed to make one another understand. I had a brother out with the army in Italy, and I think my mother hoped that if ever he was captured he would be treated as well as we treated the prisoners who worked on our farm. But he came home safely.

In 1947 we still had prisoners helping, and I remember one German, an excellent worker, who drove the tractor for me. Several times he was so engrossed in his ploughing that he forgot the time and missed the lorry back to the camp, and he'd have to walk all the way there on his own.

I brewed beer, but not cider. Made it from these 'Home Packs' you can get! My wife made nettle pop, very potent, I can tell you! But my beer! Terrible stuff! Anyone who wasn't used to it ... well, it was awful! In 1969 I brewed a lot of wine and beer and it was down the cellar for 17 years! When we moved from the Farm we brought it all up and put it in the yard. What was I to do with it? I didn't want it. A chappie came. He was used to drinking seven or eight pints a night, and he tried one of the bottles of beer. He had half a tumbler full amd couldn't get up the stairs!

Then the combine came along and made things much easier and faster. The early combines were called 'Baggers'; they bagged the grain. Later on the combines had a trailer moving alongside with a tank on it so that the grain could be taken away in bulk. An auger pumped the grain from the combine into the tank, and you didn't need to stop.

After my father died I practically lived at the Quarry; I took his seat! I got very friendly with the landlord. I've been to the Pigeon Box and Lion, but not regular. I prefered the Quarry. The pubs in the old days were a bit crude, no plush seats or anything like that, only wooden benches. They were grand places really, with grand folks. A bit on the rough side, but very friendly and genuine.

We used to play cards and dominoes. If somebody cheated, off came the jackets and fists started to fly. I used to go with Cliff Lees. One chap, Tom Gittins (who was later killed in the Grange Pit) said to us, 'You lads go and sit in the corner. I'll do your fighting for you!' We were frightened to death!

The Quarry had a choir, they sang like nightingales. If you didn't get to the pub early you'd never find a seat. Busloads from Cannock came, just to listen to them. They also had a Harvest Festival every year at the Quarry and the Vicar came too. I know the Lion put on trips for the men and had a gardening club, but I've never been involved in them.

I did go on trips to New Brighton on the Wirral with the Quarry; when there we'd go on cruises down the Mersey on the ferry *Royal Daffodil*. There'd be dancing and singing on the boat, we did have some good times, and the ladies would go along too.

As for the local bus service, Jack Jones ran it, he was a character! He had two buses, not very big ones I recall, about 26-seaters. His son Gordon drove the one and Jack would drive the other himself. I believe his other son Clive at Wrockwardine Wood drove as well in the end.

There were three pools near the Woodhouse Pit: Hangie's (Hangman's), The Rough and the Oily. The big one was the

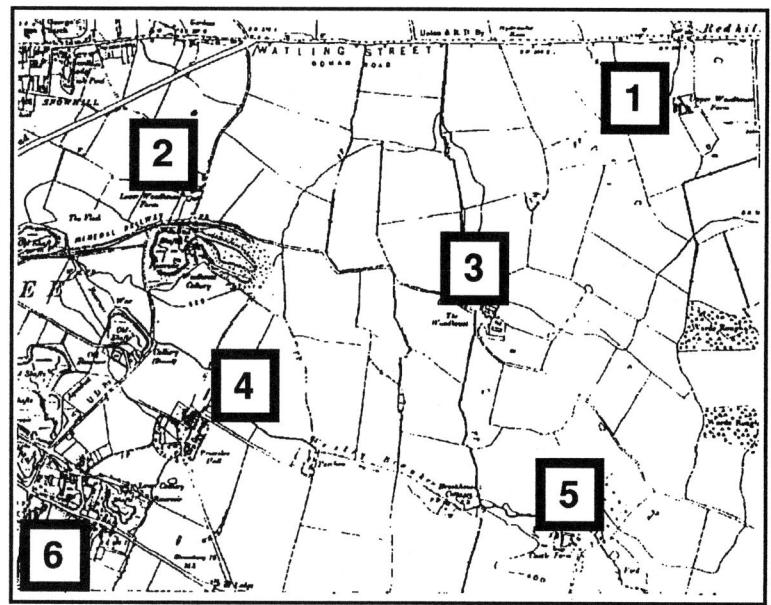

The location of farms in the Priorslee area

Key
1 Upper Woodhouse Farm
2 Lower Woodhouse Farm
3 Woodhouse Farm
4 Priorslee Hall Farm
5 Castle Farm
6 Dark Lane Farm

Hangie's, next to the main road, the Rough was over the mineral railway lines, we used to swim there. The Rough was where The Promenade is now. The Oily pool was below the Rough, separated by a track. The Oily was actually a flooded field, dug out when the new housing development started.

I've seen as many as 200 swimming in the Rough on warm Sundays in the summer! They had diving boards and the like there! The Oily was called that because of the reddish colouring from the iron ore draining out of the Pit mound. They also pumped water out of the mine at one time, using a massive machine. It was never clear water, always red.

There were good fish in the Hangie's Pool. Terrific pike. Norman Pagett caught a twenty-one pounder. It was mounted and put in the Granville Lodge club down at the furnaces for years. I don't know what happened to it, the Granville Lodge has been knocked down.

There still are a lot of pike in the pool. And roach, carp and tench. You can still fish in the pool but you have to be a member of the Telford Angling Society; they own the fishing rights to it, and the lake down by the Castle Farm Interchange, I think. I put a load of golden carp in Hangie's more than 30 years ago. I bought them off a chap who drove the milk wagon to Wolverhampton. He asked me if I wanted any, they were only four inches long, so I had fifty for about 2d each!

The Woodhouse Pit was dug for coal. I don't suppose anyone alive today can remember Hangman's working as a pit, but I think iron ore was mined there and taken down to the Lodge Brickle or Furnaces at Donnington over the A5. There was quite a deep hole on the field where Barratt Homes built their houses. I think that was caused by either sandstone or clay digging a long time ago when bricks were made down in Donnington. Before Barratt's had that field the hole was deepened by something like 12 feet when huge blocks of sandstone were taken out for building Castle Farm Way, the road to the Castle Farm Interchange. Apparently there was wet ground that needed better drainage.

We came to the Lower Woodhouse Farm in 1936. I think the Pit closed in 1940 or 1941. I suppose there were 300 or 400 men still working at the time it closed. It had become uneconomical to mine; there was plenty of coal still down there, but the men had to go too far underground to fetch it. There weren't any mining cars to carry them so they'd have to walk all the way from the shaft to the face, which could take an hour or so to do. Falls were quite common with men getting buried, sometimes fatally. There had been other accidents with explosions and falling cages or tubs going out of control.

They still had pitponies up until the closure. I think there were about 70 of them. They seldom came up alive once they were down the Pit. If they did they'd finished their working days and were put out to graze. If any were in a bad condition they were just put down. Although they were blind when they came up, their sight would eventually come back as a rule after a few weeks. There were the Old Pit Stables in 4 or 5 acres of ground around them in Priorslee Avenue, 50 yards below the Clock Tower, right alongside the road. That's where they kept the old ponies.

The Glen (the house now occupied as the doctor's surgery) was last lived in by Ernie Tranter's son Paul. Before that, Paul's grandfather lived in it. And before that, in the 1930s and during the wartime, a chap named Mr Beech lived in it when he was the Surveyor for the Pit. When Mr Beech lived there the garden was most beautiful in Springtime. All rock plants and tulips. After Church on a Sunday night folks used to walk passed it just to have a look, loads of them. I never had much to do with the church or chapel in Priorslee, only for funerals and the like. I went to the church in St Georges.

The Coal Wharf was on the other side of the road below the Pigeon Box. There was a level crossing there, and another across the main road. They used to take the coal down from the Woodhouse, the Granville and other pits to the station at Hollinswood, then distributed it on the main railway line elsewhere. Hollinswood Station wasn't really a station, more of a marshalling yard. During the War the Lilleshall Company used to sell surplus coal at the Coal Wharf. There were also railway lines going straight into the Steel Rolling Mill at Sneds Hill, and another crossing near the Greyhound pub. The Priorslee Blast Furnaces were really interesting. I remember the noise from them, which kept me awake when we first came here.

There were two blast engines for the steel mill, I think, going all night long. And when they charged up the cupolas the glow lit up the sky with an orangy-red colour. They were still working during the War, but I can't remember if they actually allowed them to work at night. I can also remember them pouring molten metal into the sand beds to make pig iron. It was hard work, moulding and puddling. They'd have to carry the bars, still warm and weighing up to a hundredweight each, with their arms protected by their aprons, from the beds, up wooden planks and into railway trucks.

Mrs Flossie Edwards managed the works canteen. It was a great place to go. I was very friendly with her son Albert. We always got fed well when we went there.

And as for the Maggot Factory! Well, it was just over the road from the works canteen. If we lost a calf it would be easier to put it into the boot of the car and take it down to the maggot factory than to dig a hole and bury it. They sold the maggots to anglers and pet shops all over the country. They put them in steel boxes before putting them on the train. The maggots were all colours; red, yellow, blue. Beautiful!

I always went to Wellington on a Thursday morning with my mother to do the banking and get the wages. One Thursday I had a calf to take to Jack Hodson so we went to drop it off on the way. We met Jack, with his greasy old pullover on, standing in the doorway to the factory. I told him what we'd got and he said to take it round the back where they did all the skinning. Oh, dear! My mother couldn't eat anything for a fortnight! The sight was disgusting and so was the smell! And the maggotmen were standing there, wrapping animals' intestines around their arms like rope!

Another time when I went down there he invited me in for a cup of tea and a sandwich. I declined!

The maggot factory closed down some five years ago, and Jack moved to near the Granville Colliery. He's now got a really smart purpose-built unit. Considering the years of protests against the terrible smell which came from the Sneds Hill factory, he's probably in the best place now. We could even smell it at the Farm. It filled the whole area when the wind was in the right (or wrong!) direction.

Mixed Memories

This final chapter is an amalgamation of memories from a variety of people with Priorslee connections. Whilst it has not always been possible to verify every revelation, and memories sometimes have a trick of confusing one event with another, the majority of information contained here has been corroborated from other sources. Obviously, tales passed down from one generation to another can simply be regarded as embelished hearsay, but nevertheless are still valid in order that the modern reader will be able to understand the conditions and circumstances which initially gave rise to those stories.

Many of the older residents can remember the overhead water troughs, suspended on iron supports and wooden posts, which came from the Lawn Pit.

The troughs followed the old mineral railway line through the Village, over some of the gardens, along the edge of the mound right by the Village (upon which a cutting had been made to support the troughs instead of using the posts unnecessarily), across the Shifnal Road high enough to allow tall vehicles to pass underneath, and finally down by the side of the road to the furnaces.

The water ran quite quickly and children often paddled in the trough on the mound, even though the water had a yellowish tinge. It is likely that the furnaces used the water as a coolant in the steel-making process, although they did have a cement works there as well later on. The sound of steam coming from there at night could often be heard. All the troughs were scrapped during the War.

The mineral lines from the Lawn and the Woodhouse Pits ran down to the Coal Wharf on the other side of a hedge by the two Company houses below the Pigeon Box. One of the two houses was a police house, possibly occupied at one time by a Mr Birdshaw. The railway lines joined one another inside the wharf. No-one was allowed in there, it was Company property. Sometimes children would sneak in and play there, but when Constable Birdshaw came and stood on the perimeter, they'd be off! The police station was later moved to Freeston Avenue.

The Lilleshall Company Drawing Office at Sneds Hill

The policemen walked the area or rode their bikes around making their presence known – and felt. Towards the end of their occupation at Priorslee they had a police car, a Wolsey with a bell on the front and an ancient handset radio.

Children often walked along the railway lines despite notices warning them that, under the Railways Acts, it was private property and trespassers would be prosecuted. T A Freeston's name was on the signs.

The Company wanted to demolish everything at the Coal Wharf, level it off and build small factory units. This was just about the time that Telford Development Corporation was created, and they refused planning permission. There is a traffic island there instead, the Priorslee Roundabout. The Corporation were also responsible for many other buildings being demolished, such as the old castle-like Company drawing office opposite where Furnace Road joins the Holyhead Road on Sneds Hill and the removal of the David and Sampson blowing engines from the furnaces to the Blists Hill Museum.

The Company never seems to have paid very good wages *(even as late as 1969 when the author worked as a fitter's mate during the college holidays he was only paid £12.00 for a 40-hour week on the night shift)*. Consequently many employees did other work to make ends meet. A few of the colliers started a form of public transport using horse-drawn wagonettes. Some made a few shillings each week by delivering fresh fish or greengrocery. In the pre-war days every penny counted.

Unfortunately the local roads were not always kept in good condition. Station Hill in Oakengates, for example, was very rough, full of holes that quickly filled with water whenever it rained. It wasn't the sort of road people liked to walk up, especially when they'd got their shopping with them. Usually they'd walk down into Oakengates and ride back. It wasn't until well after the War ended that the roads seemed to improve to any great extent.

Carrying passengers up the Greyhound Bank from Oakengates in horse-drawn wagons during the 1920s and perhaps earlier was something of an experience. As they approached the bend on the hill several passengers had to get out to give the horse a chance, and sometimes had to push as well!

Horses were excellent at knowing their own jobs. The coalmerchants' and bread delivery horses knew their customers so well that they would amble along to the next delivery and stop automatically, missing non-customers houses on the way. If a new man didn't know the route, they would!

The wagonettes used by the pioneers of public transport had a canvas roof pulled over wooden hoops. Sometimes, when it rained, the passengers pushed the canvas up from the inside, starting from the rear and working forward until the water reached the front, and the poor driver would be sitting there not knowing what was going on until they shouted out, 'All together, boys!' and they'd tip the water all over him! Rotten thing to do, but they had their fun!

The Lawn Pit ceased drawing coal sometime around the turn of the century, as did the Stafford Pit. The Lawn Engine House had a Boulton-Watt beam engine and the boilerhouse had a chimney stack and four or five boilers, but there was no cover to shelter the stokers such as there were at other boilerhouses. There were also offices and other assorted buildings and a shaft covered over with iron plates.

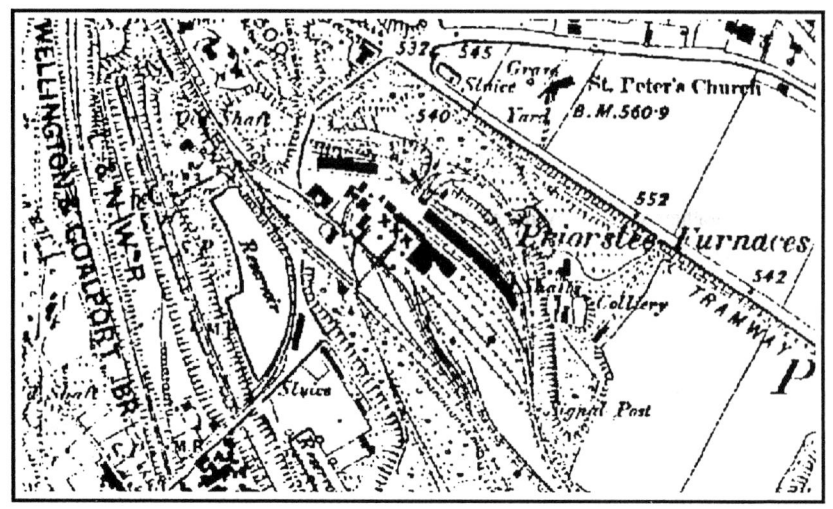

Plan of the Priorslee Furnaces area

The Priorslee Blast Furnaces, c. 1900

Even the ginny (gin-trap) that had once been turned by mules or ponies to lower men into the pit was still there in the 1920s. The ginny had a large drum in the centre with a chain coiled around it, and as the mule walked around in a circle the chain would be let out to lower a bucket containing a man down into the shaft below.

After the miners had finished their shift they'd wait their turn to be brought back to the surface – and hope the chains didn't break! Water was pumped out and carried away in the troughs to stop the water levels in the ground rising and flooding the Woodhouse mines.

Another mineral railway line ran parallel to the Shifnal Road. Trucks were often parked there when not in use. Several folk can remember there being a bee-hive shaped shelter next to the level crossing at the Coal Wharf on the Pigeon Box side. The main road from the Telford Mark roundabout joins the Priorslee Roundabout roughly where the shelter was.

An employee of the Company was paid to sit in the shelter and step outside to flag down the traffic whenever a train was due. Almost all vehicles were horse-drawn, including farm machinery, until well after the War. The gates of the two level crossings would be opened until the mineral trucks had passed over. Then the gates would be closed and the man would go back into his shelter.

That same main road follows the line of the old mineral railway northwards to the point where it branched off to the east towards the Woodhouse Pit. There was once a mound by the mineral line where corn was grown, but in 1915 it apparently sank down and became a pool. This was probably caused by mining subsidence. During dry summers it was possible to see the old fence posts, which had surrounded the field, sticking up out of the water.

One of the other pools to the south of the Woodhouse Pit was said to have had two pit shafts in the middle of it; whether this was the place where Woodhouse Number 2 Pit was, or some other unnamed pit from years before, is not known. Old men said folk weren't to go swimming there because it was too dangerous.

The Corporation bulldozed the surrounding mounds away and filled in the pool, and at the same time created an artificial mound planted with trees on the western end of the Flash where the mineral line had been. Perhaps it was to shield St Georges and Sneds Hill from the new estates. Or vice versa. Or both. They also amalgamated the Flash and the 'Rough' to form one complete pool with an island in the middle, a good thing for the wildlife.

Years ago everyone went swimming in the oblong pool (the 'Rough') where the water was clear. There weren't any public baths they could go to – and it was free! There was a little pump house with a small boiler on the embankment next to it and the water seemes to have been circulated constantly.

The square-shaped reservoir at the Lawn Pit had a pinkish colour to it, probably the result of ironstone in the proximity. It, too, was used for occasional swimming by local youths.

Several people have mentioned that one of the pit mounds near the Village sank about 10 feet around 1950. It was thought that there had been a large cavern-like hole underneath supported by oak pitprops, apparently where the pit ponies had been kept when the pit there was working, and the ground above collapsed. The rumblings could be heard as far away as the Pigeon Box. Oak pitprops were reckoned to last up to 100 years before they were no longer safe, or as safe as anything could be in the mines.

Long ago the Village was a fairly small place with a few large houses and a couple of rows of labourers' cottages. Stable Row wasn't a stable at all, just labourers' cottages remodelled after the Corporation came. Another row, no longer there, had wash-houses at the back. The actual stable was down the road below the Clock Tower. It was quite large and had a porch for the blacksmith to do his work. Apparently there was also a fully equipped blacksmith's shop and forge on the Shifnal Road.

One of the local bus companies was J Jones and Sons, sometimes known as Priory Motors, which was based in the Village and served the area for many years. Like several other similar companies belonging to the Shropshire Omnibus Association based at Oakengates they began by using horse-drawn vehicles. These companies not only provided local passenger services to places like St Georges, Oakengates, Donnington and, later, Wellington, but also laid on special excursions for the general public to places further afield.

The Lilleshall Company logo

Practically every man in Priorslee worked full time at the Pits, the furnaces or another of the Lilleshall Company's industrial interests. If they didn't, they wouldn't have been able to have a house here. Virtually everything in the area belonged to or was leased by the Lilleshall Company.

The Woodhouse Pit was lit up at night with electric lights powered by the pit's own generator and boilers which may also have supplied the Hall besides, in later years, operating the winding gear over the shafts.

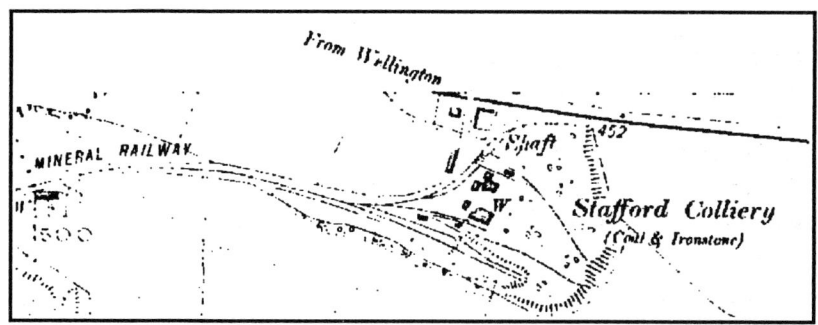

Plan of the Stafford Pits, c. 1889

Plans of the Lawn Pit and the two Woodhouse Collieries may be seen on page 57.

There were two pits at the Woodhouse – Number 1 and Number 2, but Number 2 closed down years before Number 1, perhaps as a result of action during the General Strike or because it became uneconomic; it, too, had winding gear.

The job of Banksman at the Pits partly involved tidying up all the dirt and rubbish from the mine. The stokers were only allowed very poor grade coal slack mixed with dirt to heat the boilers, and the steam pressure had to be maintained all the time. They also had to look after the pumps and the large fans used for ventilating the shafts. If anything had failed or pressure was allowed to reduce, the methane gases in the pits would have built up. And then, of course, a little spark could have proved disastrous. It is thought that the engines at The Woodhouse Pit were sold as scrap during the War.

There were a lot of old pits in the whole area, including Sneds Hill and St Georges, most without a name. Geological maps show a highly complex structure of faulted coal seams in this part of the East Shropshire Coalfield, where the tendency was for shallower seams to be found in the south-western and western end of the Field and gradually getting much deeper towards the east and northeast.

These pits around Priorslee wouldn't have lasted very long because the seams were too narrow and difficult to extract. Even old Ordnance Survey maps don't show every one, so there could be several unsuspecting folk with a mine shaft beneath their living room. It is doubtful that their title deeds allow them to extract coal for their own use, especially in a smokeless zone!

Miners were always given a metal token, numbered individually and stamped with the name of the pit and the company which owned it, when they reported for work each day. When they came back to the surface they handed the token in at the pit office as confirmation that they had safely returned. Anyone caught abusing this essential safety precaution would be fined or dismissed.

An example of these tokens is given on page 58.

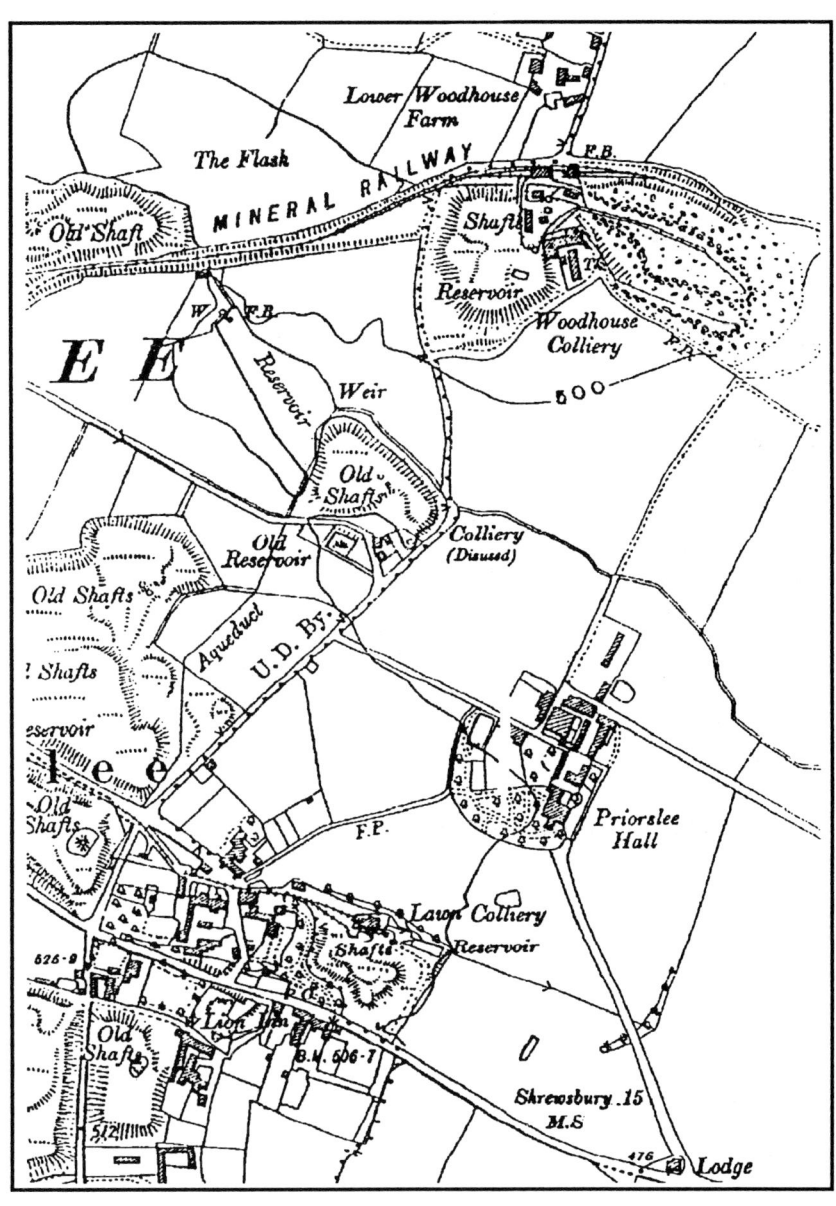

Priorslee in 1938

*Miner's Token from
the Stafford Pit*